Sailor's Start-Up:

A Beginner's Guide to Sailing
2nd Edition

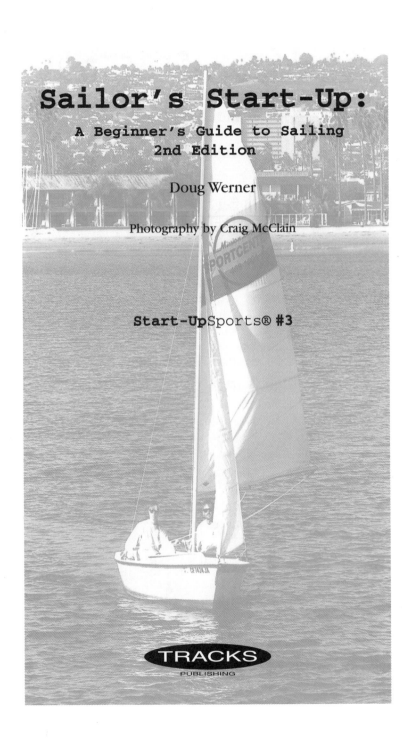

Sailor's Start-Up:

A Beginner's Guide to Sailing
2nd Edition

Doug Werner

Photography by Craig McClain

Start-Up Sports® **#3**

TRACKS
PUBLISHING

Sailor's Start-Up:

A Beginner's Guide to Sailing
2nd Edition

Doug Werner

Photography by Craig McClain

Start-Up Sports® / Tracks Publishing
140 Brightwood Avenue
Chula Vista, CA 91910
619-476-7125 Fax 619-476-8173

Copyright © 1994, 2001 by Doug Werner
FIRST edition 1994
Second printing 1994
Third printing 1997
Fourth printing, SECOND edition 2001

Publisher's Cataloging in Publication

Werner, Doug, 1950-
    Sailor's start-up : a beginner's guide to sailing /
Doug Werner. – 2nd ed.
    p. cm. – (Start-up sports ; #3)
    Includes bibliographical references and index.
    LCCN: 2001116835
    ISBN: 1-884654-01-0

    1. Sailing. I. Title. II. Series.

GV811.W44 2001   797.1'24
                        QBI01-200322

To
Mom and Dad

Acknowledgements:

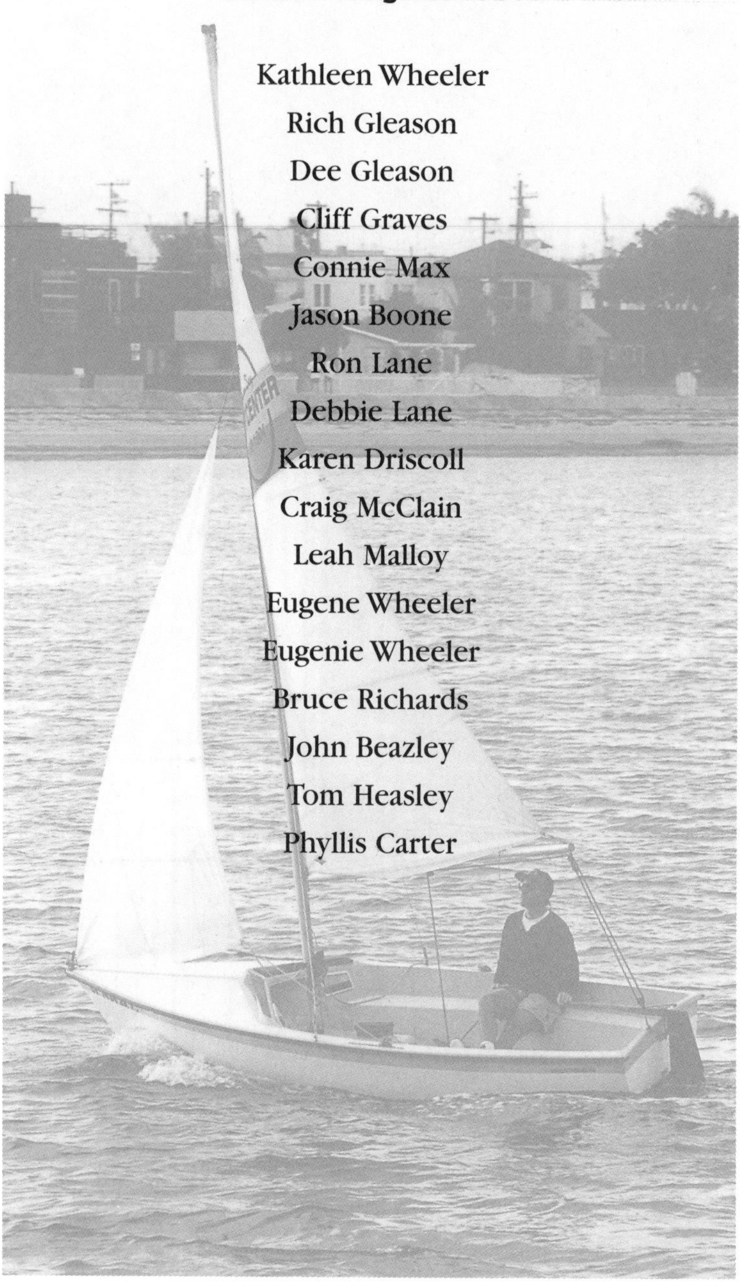

Kathleen Wheeler

Rich Gleason

Dee Gleason

Cliff Graves

Connie Max

Jason Boone

Ron Lane

Debbie Lane

Karen Driscoll

Craig McClain

Leah Malloy

Eugene Wheeler

Eugenie Wheeler

Bruce Richards

John Beazley

Tom Heasley

Phyllis Carter

Joy

I moved to San Diego in 1980 and among the first things I did after securing a job was to buy a sailboat. It was a nifty little thing that could barely be roped atop my 1965 VW Squareback. Trips to the water were frequent and frightful but we made it without a hitch every time.

Off Fiesta Island I taught myself how to sail and had the time of my life. That summer and fall I sailed Mission Bay, San Diego Bay (chased from the carriers parked at North Island Naval Base), and even made gusty runs into open ocean.

I took a friend sometimes but I best remember sailing by myself — relieved to be out there and exhilarated to be able to expertly tear along with the wind. I'd look at the busy world on shore and feel so very removed from it all.

A special place, the open waters. And sailing is a special thing to do upon them — riding the wind without a care in the world. This book is written in the spirit of joy and freedom that sailing is.

Sail safe and sail fun. Get out there!

Doug Werner

Contents:

Preface   7
Introduction   11

Chapter 1   What to wear   15
Chapter 2   The right boat   17
Chapter 3   Parts   21
Chapter 4   Conditions   29
Chapter 5   Classwork   33
Chapter 6   Launch!   37
Chapter 7   On a reach   43
Chapter 8   Downwind sailing   51
Chapter 9   Upwind sailing   57
Chapter 10   Docking   63
Chapter 11   Rules of the road   69
Chapter 12   Physics   77
Chapter 13   Rigging and knots   81
Chapter 14   Safety   95
Chapter 15   Bligh syndrome   97
Chapter 16   Catamarans   101
Chapter 17   Tacking in a cat   111
Chapter 18   How cats go   117

Glossary   123
Resources   127
Bibliography   135
Index   137

A place to begin

If you have never sailed, these questions are pop-popping in your head, or should be:

1. What do I wear?
2. What do I sail in?
3. What are the parts of the boat?
4. Where do I sail?
5. How do I set up the boat?
6. How do I leave the dock?
7. How do I make it go the way I want?
8. Where are the brakes?

Simple questions deserve simple answers. If the philosophy is to have fun, and the goal is to get out in the water right away — the method had better be simple or you'll get hung up in the classroom. Or worse, reading a book like this!

Instruction
This book will get you started and become a resource as you fumble about during your first days. But real-live instruction is practically irreplaceable. A good teacher has a much better chance to impart knowledge, inspire confidence and imprint the sailing experience than mere words on paper.

You can learn from a friend or relative but that's not always a great idea. Strange things happen between intimate folks when one or the other becomes *Coach*. Just because someone's a great mom or dad or chum or mate as well as a good sailor does not mean he will be a good instructor.

Learn from a professional. They've done it before a thousand times. They know how to do it right and they know how to deal with yearlings like you. Any place that has sailing has instruction somewhere. Ask around and shop around. It'll be a good investment (although it shouldn't cost much), and an education (one in which you'll actually learn something).

It's an opportunity to rub shoulders with authentic sailing people in their natural habitat and to learn with others like you. Take a class. They're cheaper than private lessons and there's bound to be someone just as inept as you.

So why the book? Even the best instruction may not cover things adequately for you. You'll forget things or remain confused about this or that. Instruction also comes and goes. The book is a reference that'll stick around for a while and makes an excellent coaster when you're through with it.

Get out there!
Sailing is many, many things. It's a hobby. It's a sport. It's an intellectual pursuit. It's a passion. It's a social thing. It's an individual thing. It's complicated. It's simple. It's relaxing. It's exciting. It's a labor. It's a labor of love. It's poetic, popular, yet vaguely elitist. It's ancient, eternal

and silly in some ways. But front page, futuristic and hip as well.

This book is about getting started and getting out there. Simple, straightforward. No long diatribes about theory. No baffling passages of nautical jargon and strategies. No long-winded explanations of why, what, and how. Just what you need to know.

Ready to go!

Chapter 1:
What to wear

The boat you *should* be in will not tip over easily so you needn't worry about getting wet. Dress like you would if you were just strolling the water's edge — warm or cool enough so that you're comfortable.

Hat with visor or brim
The sun is bad news. If you're thinning on top, caps are a must.

Sunglasses
Unless you enjoy viewing the waterscape in a whiteout with a headache, wear eye protection — with a strap.

Sunscreen
The water magnifies sunny conditions.

Sneakers
You'll be scrambling so something with a grip is required.

Life preservers
This is the law. One for each sailor. Not necessarily worn but in the boat.

As you progress and try tippier boats you will capsize. You'll need to consider wet suits or dry suits in cooler water and weather — but that's later.

Chapter 2:
The right boat

One of the major factors involved in happy beginnings.

Sailboats are like cars, computers and portable heaters — there are a billion makes and models. What makes sailboats different is that boat builders have had 2,000 years or so to refine the confusion.

But the right boat for you is easy to describe and easy to find. I suggest a 14-foot monohull. Monohull means one hull, as opposed to two (or three), like a cata-maran. It's a model that's available most places that have sailing. They are built by several different manu-facturers the world over.

These boats are big enough for up to four people, yet quite manageable for one. The common version is wide and steady (it won't capsize easily), simple to rig and easy to handle. They are also relatively inexpensive and reliable (they last forever). In short, they're a good, basic sailboat for all levels of expertise.

A 14-foot monohull is perfect for beginners.

Stay away from anything much bigger. There's usually more stuff to confuse and they can be intimidating. It's less frightening to feel out of control on a 14-foot boat than a 22-foot boat.

Smaller boats are OK but avoid the tippy ones. Certain models may seem dorky or too cramped for adults. You want something that's comfy enough to spend some time in, steady enough that you can concentrate on your sailing, and dry enough that you don't have to worry about getting wet.

Learn the basics in a monohull. Catamarans are sexy but a bit tricky. Learn how to walk, then you can fly. Mind you, this is a vast simplification of what's what in sailboats — but simple is good for now.

Rent
Find a place that rents. That way all you have to do is show up in your yachting ensemble. No trailers, no ramps, no parking your boat in the alley. Buy when you know more and you're sure you want to try backing boat and trailer into the garage.

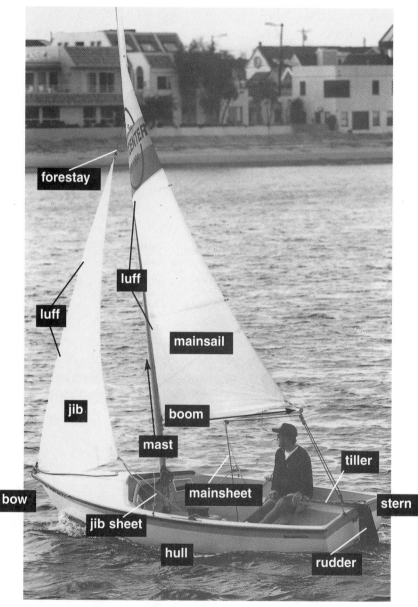

Basic sailboat parts

Chapter 3:
Parts

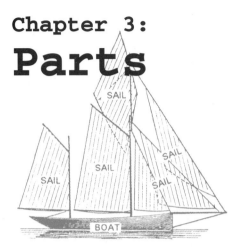

This is your boat
Sailboats are simple once you get down to basics.

Sails
Every sailboat has at least one sail. Our boat has two —
a big one called a mainsail and a little one called a jib. A
boat with this configuration is called a sloop. The way
sails work is interesting, but we'll get into theory later.

Why two sails? More sail means more area for the
wind, which means faster sailing. You don't need two
sails. Just make sure you have one.

Mast
And every sailboat has one of these. It holds up the
sails.

Boom
This is the wooden or metal beam attached to the mast
and the bottom of the mainsail. It stabilizes the sail. It's
called a boom because it swings back and forth when

you turn. If it hits you, it goes boom!

Sheets

Not the billowy part of the sails. Strangely enough, this is the name for the ropes attached to the sails. The sheets allow you to adjust the tension in the sails, which in turn helps adjust the speed of your boat. The mainsheet sprouts from a swivel gizmo (cleat) in the middle and bottom of the hull. The jib has two sheets, angling in from cleats on either side of the boat.

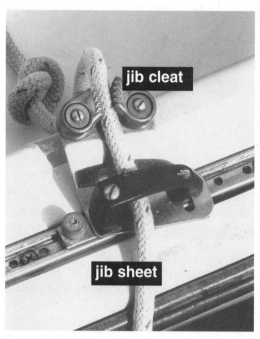

jib cleat

jib sheet

Cleats

The gizmos that tie down the sheets have teeth that always let you pull in. The teeth prevent the sails from pulling out. A yank up or down frees the sheet. A yank the other way sets the teeth.

Daggerboard or centerboard

This is the thing jutting out from underneath the boat. If it pops in and out, it's called a daggerboard. If it pivots, it's called a centerboard. Both serve the same functions. They stabilize the craft and play a major role

daggerboard

in the physics of sailing. Just remember you need one or the other.

Tiller and rudder

The tiller is your steering wheel and the rudder acts as your tires. You hold on to the tiller which is attached to the rudder. The rudder is the part in the water. Push or pull one way and you turn in the opposite direction. Don't even try to visualize it. Once you get out there it'll come together without much thought.

Hull
The boat part of the boat.

Luff
Believe it or not, there are up to a dozen parts to a sail. For now just commit this to memory: The luff is the leading edge of the jib and mainsails. The luff indicates sail tension.

mainsheet

jib sheet

Parts

shrouds

starboard

port

Telltails and shrouds
Telltails are strips of fabric attached to the sails or to the shrouds on either side of the boat. They indicate wind direction. Shrouds are the wires that hold up the mast.

Bow
The front of the boat.

Stern
The back of the boat.

Port
As you face forward inside your boat, this is the left side.

Starboard
The right side.

You know, even if someone had an explanation for these last two terms (I refuse to research it) there is little defense for the use of these words. I can't think of any other human endeavor that deliberately confuses the left and right. I mean, this is ridiculous! Along with green pasta, detergent commercials and California's incomprehensible sales tax laws.

No sheet! or Introducing The Code
Grab the sheet! he shouted as our boat headed into the first leg of the race.

I was along for fun, in a "fun" race, although I knew nothing about sailing and less about sailing terminology — as I was about to prove.

We were tacking around the first marker and the boom had just swung around. Sails were flapping and ropes were every-which-way, as is the case before you set the sails. It was my job to man the jib. Easy enough, really. Just uncleat the rope on one side of the boat and cleat the rope on the other side when the boat turns, or tacks, and the boom swoops around. That's what I was about to do when the skipper bellowed instructions about the sheet.

The sheet! Grab the sheet! Pull in the sheet NOW! he barked.

Not wanting to hesitate in the thick of it, I went after what had to be the sheet. Sheets are either fabric or paper, right? I mean that's how it comes. In sheets. The only thing close to that were the sails. Sheets. Sails. That's gotta be it! So I leapt up onto the bow and wrestled with the jib. *Got it! Now what?* I yelled as I stumbled and grasped.

What are you doing! Mr. Skip answered in a not so pleasant way. *Get down here and pull in the sheet!*

Somewhat dismayed and confused, I managed to regain my seat in the hull. *What's a sheet?* I asked.

The rope! This rope! he exclaimed grabbing one of the ropes attached to the jib and cleating it down. The same job I was about to do before all this sheet stuff started. Well, of course. A sheet is a rope. How stupid of me.

By this time we are out of the race. All the loose sheets,

my dance on the bow and my verbal ineptitude had cost us dearly. We came in dead last. As we approached the dock, the cat calls began.

I thought it was pretty funny, but Captain Ahab didn't. He proceeded to explain things to me in a faintly authoritarian manner (this is a symptom of a common personality disfunction associated with sailing that will be explored soon) — as if any sort of explanation could excuse calling a rope a sheet.

That was my first experience with The Code.

And it's something you better get used to because like it or not it's a big part of sailing. I work around it in this book in order to simplify things, but beware that in the strange, yet real world of docks, marinas and clubs, the names for things don't make sense. It's a linguistic conspiracy among sailors the world over. For lack of a better term we will call this puzzling cultural trait — The Code.

Conditions

Perfect — slight wind and no traffic.

Chapter 4:
Conditions

You need the right boat and you need the right conditions to learn in. The boat you know about ...

Water
You can sail on lakes, rivers, bays and oceans. The common denominator is water. The place you learn should be deep enough to allow for your daggerboard or centerboard. Sounds obvious but even old salts find themselves high and dry once in a while because they didn't know the bottom. Learn where sandbars, reefs, sunken wrecks and ancient cities are located before casting off. And pick a place that isn't swarming with traffic. You're going to be sailing wild and loose for a while — make sure there's plenty of room.

As a rule, a good place to begin is a small, enclosed bay or cove off a larger body of water. Winds are usually lighter in such places than over an open expanse. You'll not be dealing with waves, shipping lanes, dangerous currents or migrating whales, either.

A flying hull indicates a stiff wind — not beginner-friendly conditions.

Wind

Look at the other sailboats already out and about. How are they moving along? If catamaran hulls are flying (lifting out of the water), the wind is too much for you. If the boats are sailing at a more moderate pace — go for it. A very light wind is fine. Just make sure the sailors and their vessels are actually moving.

No boats? Check out the chop. If there are whitecaps, the wind is at least 12 knots and that's too strong. The higher the chop, the greater the wind. Flags can help, of course. An expert opinion at this point is a very good idea.

The thing is, you don't want to learn in difficult conditions. Right now it's easy does it — mild winds with just enough push in a safe, secluded patch of water.

Chapter 5:
Classwork

You won't learn it until you do it, but there is a bit of lore to know before setting out. Sailing is all about wind — wind determines all your moves.

Wind circle *(Illustration 5a, next page)*
This doesn't look like fun. Here you thought you'd be reading about billowing sails and spray-in-your-face, and instead you get this — something out of high-school geometry.

You can't sail directly into the wind (upwind). In fact, you can't sail under 45 degrees to either side. This is called the **dead zone**. If you're pointed into the dead zone, you come to a dead stop.

Despite its name, the dead zone is very important and useful when you turn and dock the boat. It's also a good place to be pointed when in trouble or just confused — because that's where the brakes are!

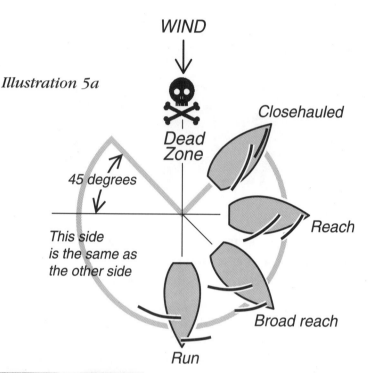

Illustration 5a

WIND

Closehauled

Dead Zone

45 degrees

Reach

This side is the same as the other side

Broad reach

Run

Understanding points of sail may come easier in the boat than in the classroom. Cliff and Connie are pointed into the wind and stalled. Hence the name of this point of sail — the dead zone.

Wind circle — Indicated in the illustration above are the directions you can sail and their proper names. These are called **points of sail**. The left side of the circle is the same as the right. All direction is determined by **wind source**. It makes perfect sense on the water.

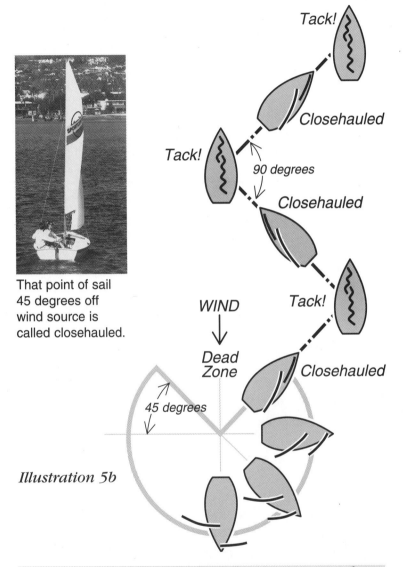

Tack!

Closehauled

Tack!

90 degrees

Closehauled

WIND

Tack!

Dead
Zone

Closehauled

45 degrees

Illustration 5b

That point of sail
45 degrees off
wind source is
called closehauled.

Tacking — From the **wind circle** you zigzag in **close-hauled** courses and 90 degree, upwind turns called **tacks**. The zigs and zags are necessary in order to sail around the dead zone. This is the only way to reach an upwind bearing in a sailboat.

Although sailing stops in the dead zone, everywhere else on the circle you'll move:

Closehauled is as close to upwind you can travel.

Reaching is sailing 90 degrees to wind direction.

Running is sailing with the wind (downwind).

Broad reaching is sailing in between reaching and running.

All these directions are called **points of sail**.

Tacking *(Illustration 5b)*
This is awful, isn't it? But get a grip. This is the hardest part.

It's easy to go left and right and down.

The stickler is going up, as in upwind. Somehow you have to zig and zag around the dead zone. All this zigging and zagging is called **tacking**. It looks like turning — and that's what it is.

The trick to tacking involves switching the sides that you and the sails have been operating.

That's a wrap for now. Let's go sailing.

Chapter 6: Launch!

Leaving the dock

First things first. Which way is the wind blowing? Remember the wind circle. You cannot sail into the wind or less than 45 degrees to either side. So make sure the wind is coming from the side or from behind your boat. If it isn't, you must walk, paddle or tow your boat into such a position so that it is. The direction you're headed should be toward open water and clear sailing.

1 Determine which side of the boat the mainsail and boom will be before you board. Unless you're pointed upwind, the mainsail will want to be on one side or the other. You don't have to force the issue.

Ready? A bunch of things will happen at once. If you have some help pushing off, you can settle in first. And if you have a boating companion you can split the chores.

2 Untie the boat and push off the dock with one foot. Step toward the center of the boat, next to the mast, with the other.

Launch!

Launch — Cliff holds the boat steady as Tom settles at the tiller. The boat is positioned so winds will take it to open water.

Cliff steps into the middle of the boat next to the mast. At the same time he pushes off the dock with the other foot.

Tom steers the boat into open water ...

... and pulls in the mainsheet.

5

Cliff reaches for the jib sheet in order to adjust the jib sail.

6

Note that Tom is always looking ahead, always has a hand on the tiller and always has hold of the mainsheet.

7

Trimming adjustments are made on the jib and mainsail. Both Cliff and Tom seek to make taut foils of their sails.

8

The way is clear. Away they go.

3 Settle in next to the tiller opposite the sail and grab hold of the tiller and the mainsheet.

4 Pull in the mainsheet just enough to get going.

5 As the sail fills, steer clear of the docking area. Pick a point on the opposite shore and aim for it. This is called setting a bearing.

6 By now the jib is flapping (luffing), so pull it in with the jib sheet on the same side as the mainsail and cleat it down.

If you've been counting, in the span of five seconds or so you have been asked to grapple with three things (tiller, mainsheet and jib sheet) with only two hands. Pretty tricky, huh? Not to mention the scrambling around and the guy on the dock shouting at you incoherently.

Now is an excellent time to panic, but don't. If you must, let the jib flap away for a bit and just concentrate on handling the mainsail and steering out to open water. Do set it, though, as soon as you can.

All the juggling becomes more manageable as you clock more sailing time. It's like driving a stick shift for the first time — you may feel confused and awkward, but try to relax and go with the flow. You'll get it soon enough. Just stay away from everybody and everything until you do!

OK. Back to your initial trim.

Trimming

taut sails = trim

Trimming your sails is all about pulling in on the sheets until the sails stop flapping. What you want are nice taut foils of sail. This tautness indicates proper sail tension. The first and last part of the sails to flap are the luffs or leading edges of both jib and mainsails. Hence the luffs are terrific checkpoints for adjusting sail tension and trim.

When in doubt — *let 'em out!*

To find proper sail trim at any point after you've set a bearing, let your sails out until they flap or luff. (Yes, the word *luff* can be a subject or a verb and sometimes at the same time.) Then pull 'em in until you have those full, wrinkle-free foils. The look and feel of properly trimmed sails is something you'll pick up fairly quickly with practice, and is definitely one of the major sweet spots in sailing.

So you've pulled in your jib and cleated it down. And you've pulled in your mainsail. Don't cleat this one because trimming is a constant thing. At this point you're holding the mainsheet with one hand and the tiller with the other — steering toward the bearing you set earlier.

This is your sailing posture — one hand monitors the

sail and one hand steers the boat. You've got an eye on your sails as well as the water around you — all the time.

Hey! You're sailing!

Slicing along without gas fumes, noise or traffic lights. Pretty neat, huh? Just like John Paul Jones and Chris Columbus.

By now you've discovered why you sit where you do. The sail wants to pull one way so sitting on the opposite side balances things out. This is trimming the boat itself. Of course the other reason for sitting there is to *see*. The sail is in your face otherwise.

Scoot up or back to achieve the proper trim fore (front) and aft (back). You want the boat to cut level through the water.

Chapter 7:

On a reach

Reach —The wind is blowing into Cliff's back — 90 degrees to the length of the boat. Sails are about half out. Note the full foil shape of each sail.

Let's discover the reality of the wind circle. Actually, at this point you've already found out about a piece of it, since you've no doubt been on a reach or thereabouts since you left the dock.

A reach is sailing at right angles to the wind. That's probably your position because it's the optimum direction for sail and boat trim as well as speed. It's the natural notch to slide into. The telltails on your shrouds should be streaming at a 90 degree angle to the length of the boat.

Stay on this course awhile. Get a feel for the lift of the boat, the tug of the sheet and sail, and the tiller in your hand. Sailing is about balancing those things and it really does boil down to feel. There's no computerized gizmo to guide you and who would want it! Half the charge of sailing is seeking the forces that move you and tapping into that energy.

As you dial into the lifts and tugs notice they change. That's because the wind isn't a constant. It usually blows in gusts. On the same heading or bearing you'll constantly adjust sail tension. Puffs of wind will hit and away you'll go — sometimes so hard the sail will pull your boat way over. In that case, let out the sail.

On a reach you pull in to gain speed and let out to slow down. Turn the boat toward the dead zone (upwind) if need be. That'll settle things down. Conversely, in order to speed up, reel in your sheets and make sure your telltails are sideways into the sail.

Why does the boat speed up on a reach? Why does pulling in or letting out the sail make the boat go fast and slow? An explanation requires some theoretical song and dance. There's a chapter on that ahead.

Capsized!
One of these days you're going to capsize. It happens to everybody who sails small boats. It has always happened to me on a reach — when I've set my sails too tight and the wind just blew me over.

Getting upright is usually no big deal. Normally when a sailboat capsizes, it's lying on its side with the mast and sails floating on top of the water. After you've resurfaced from your dunking, swim over to the boat and uncleat the sheets. You don't want the sails to act as buckets when you rock the boat upright. Also, a boat with sheets cleated will take off as soon as it's erect. This is very important because chances are you won't be in the boat yet.

Paddle over to the centerboard which should be sticking out like a platform. Scramble up on it and grab the side of the boat. As you stand up, the boat should right itself without much fuss. Unless, of course, something unusual is underfoot...

Mast-in-mud incident
As is the normal course of events for calamity, this mishap occurred when I was trying to impress someone. It was my date's first time on a sailboat and I was going to teach her how to sail. This, by the way, is a tried and true mating ritual wherever sails are unfurled.

So off we went in my boat. It was cozy because we were in an itty-bitty Laser. Lasers are squirrely, zippy, and tippy. A real blast if you don't mind getting wet. We zoomed along for a while in a moderate wind, just having a high old time.

Lasers like to pop their hulls way up out of the water when a gust hits on a reach. What you do then is hook your feet underneath the hiking strap in the cockpit and lean out over the water in order to compensate for the sail, which is pulling the other way. It can be a real bronco ride and successfully executing those hikes can really impress a pretty passenger.

Capsize recovery — Sheets are released immediately. Otherwise the sails would act as giant buckets.

Cliff grabs hold of the centerboard and pulls down.

Tom comes over to help.

It isn't always easy!

Here we go!

The sails finally pop free and the hull settles upright.

It should be noted that capsizing doesn't happen often in a boat of this type. It actually took longer to tip the boat over than it did to right it.

Until you capsize.

Like I said, Lasers are tippy and capsizing is part of the game when you max out on a reach. But, hey. So we got a little wet. No harm done. The water was warm, we were in our suits, and flipping the thing upright would be a snap. Just uncleat the sheet, stand on the centerboard, and presto! We'd be back in business.

Something, however, was odd. Usually when you dump, the boat floats sideways on the water. The sail lays flat on the water, preventing the boat from turning all the way over. Yet this time the centerboard was thrusting straight up. The sail was nowhere to be seen. My little boat was completely upside down.

Trying not to display any concern, I reached up, got a grip on my centerboard and tried to yank the ship over. Not a budge.

I planted my feet on the hull and tried again. Nada.

Glancing at my crew, I noticed that her nervous look had changed to a squinty grimace that typically indicates the onset of panic.

This was grim. My manhood was at stake! It was time for assertion. Action. Heroics, even. I dove down along the mast to discover that its tip was buried in a foot of mud. I resurfaced after a bit of digging to report back and catch a breath.

She stared wide-eyed at my muddiness extremus and seemed to have difficulty registering my reassurances.

I'm sure all she heard was the part about *digging the mast out of the bottom of the bay*.

I returned to my buried mast and this time managed to free it. I pushed it back to the surface, hopped back onto the centerboard, and with a grunt, hauled the sucker up and over. We pulled ourselves back into the boat, I reset the sail, and away we putted.

My date? Well, she lost her evil eye, heaved an unmistakable sigh of relief, and finally gave me an oh-my-hero look. She sat very close and patted my leg. The old rescue-the-damsel-in-distress routine (never mind that I provided the distress). Works every time.

Running — The wind is blowing directly over the stern of the boat. The sails are adjusted all the way out.

In the first photo, the jib and mainsail are set on opposite sides to maximize sail area. However, as is often the case, the jib fizzles and only the main remains.

Chapter 8:
Downwind
sailing

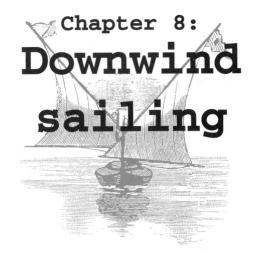

Sailing with the wind (downwind) is perhaps the eas-
iest direction to maintain in light to moderate wind.
Oddly enough, it's about the slowest way to go, and
since you set your sail just one way when you travel
downwind, there's next to zero adjustments to make
along the way.

Turn downwind and let out your sails. All the way. Your
telltails should be streaming straight ahead. Adjust the
mainsail so that it sticks out 90 degrees to the boat.
Chances are your jib won't even work because the
mainsail is in the way. You can try sheeting the jib on
the opposite side to the main, but it may or may not do
much. Hold it right there and whistle a tune. That's all
there is to it.

You're wondering how come a sailboat sails so slow
going with the wind, right? It seems that it ought to be
the swiftest path. There is a reason and it will be given
soon enough.

Jibing *(Illustration 8a, next page)*

A faster way to travel downwind involves sailing in a series of zigzags toward your downwind bearing. Although this course is longer, since you're angling downwind on a broad reach, it's faster than sailing directly downwind.

As you can see, this zigzagging requires changing direction or turning at certain intervals. The turn used in downwind sailing is called a jibe. Simply put, jibing is pulling the tiller toward you.

Jibes are a little tricky because the sails catch the wind very quickly as you turn. The boom swings around fast and can catch you unprepared. In a strong wind, a jibe can really jolt you and the boat — not a good thing.

1 Before you do anything, look in the direction you want to go and **see that the way is clear.**

2 **Make sure you're pointed on a broad reach.** Never jibe from a reach. You do not want to go into a jibe with too much speed.

3 **Pull the tiller toward you.**

4 **Release both sails** (uncleat jib and mainsails).

5 **Switch sides** and duck as the boom swings over.

6 **Set your sails** (cleat jib and haul in main).

7 **Find your broad reach** course and get a bearing on the shore.

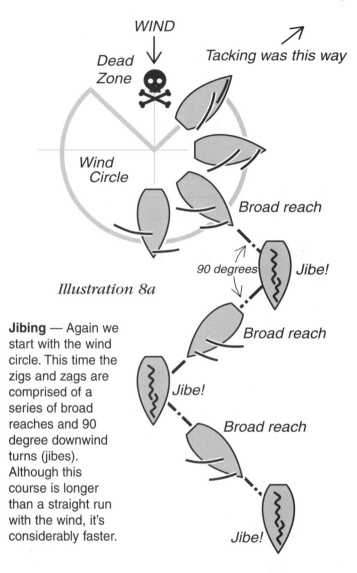

Illustration 8a

Jibing — Again we start with the wind circle. This time the zigs and zags are comprised of a series of broad reaches and 90 degree downwind turns (jibes). Although this course is longer than a straight run with the wind, it's considerably faster.

With practice, you'll get a feel for this maneuver and the rhythm of sailing on a broad reach, making a jibe, sailing on a broad reach, making a jibe, and so on. Remember easy-does-it with jibing. The wind will pick you up lickity-split as you turn. Be prepared!

Downwind sailing

Jibing — Cliff and Connie begin a jibe from a broad reach.

Cliff slowly pulls the tiller toward him.

As the boat swings around ...

... all eyes are on the boom.

This is the critical part. The wind is blowing over the stern and will catch the mainsail at any moment.

Cliff and Connie release the sheets ... and the wind catches the main. As the boom swoops overhead, they switch sides.

Cliff and Connie adjust and trim the sails to suit the new course. Note that Cliff has hold of the tiller throughout the sequence maintaining a steady course.

Closehauled — The boat is sailing as close to an upwind direction as possible. Straight upwind is just off to Cliff's left or port. Sails are hauled in close (get it?) in order to maximize trim.

Chapter 9:
Upwind sailing

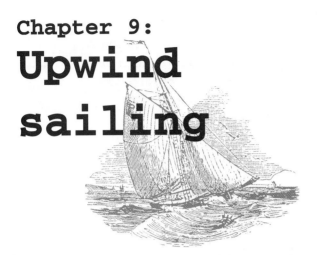

Remember that frightening diagram in the classroom chapter? The one with all the zigzags coming out of the wind circle? Well, that's the symbology of sailing into the wind — the art of sailing closehauled and tacking.

(Oh, by the way. Although one may say reach*ing*, run-n*ing* and broad reach*ing*, one cannot say closehaul*ing*. There is no present participle for this particular point of sail. Why? The Code!)

Sailing closehauled

The reality of that diagram is a lot easier to understand in a boat. Put yourself into a reach. Now slowly steer the boat into the wind until you see the luff of the jib begin to flap. As soon as you do, turn the boat ever so slightly back again just so that sail tension is regained. You are now sailing closehauled, 45 degrees off the wind source — as close as a sailor can get to the dead zone and still move. As close as a sailor can ever get to sailing upwind.

Since you're headed upwind at best at a 45 degree angle, in order to reach an upwind bearing you must execute a series of 90 degree turns to get there. Hence all the zigzagging. The zigs and zags are sailed close-hauled. Turning into a zig or zag is called a tack.

Tacking

Tacking is pushing the tiller away from you and turning the boat until the sail and boom swing around and catch the wind from the other side. Sounds simple, and it is in theory, but there's a trick or two.

First, try a tack from a reach. You'll have more speed to turn you through the dead zone.

1. **Look** and make sure you're not turning into a party boat.

2. **Build up your speed.**

3. **Push the tiller away** from you.

4. **Release both sails** (uncleat jib and mainsail).

5. **Switch sides and duck** as the boom swings around.

6. **Set your sails** (cleat jib and haul in main).

7. **Find your closehauled course** and get a bearing on the shore.

Got all that? Don't sweat it. This takes practice. Tacking is like learning how to turn on skis or a snowboard. It's

Beginning a tack — Cliff starts his turn from a closehauled course by pushing the tiller away.

Tacking — The boat is pointed directly into the dead zone.

Cliff maintains his turn on the tiller.

As the boat swings around they switch sides ...

... and adjust sails.

Backwinding — The boat is stopped in the dead zone. Connie pushes the main sail out to catch some wind.

While Connie holds the sail out, Cliff pulls the tiller over. The boat begins to back into a turn.

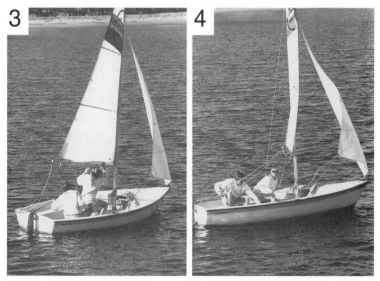

Finally the boat backs into a point of sail. Connie quickly seats herself as the main sail catches and the boom swings around.

somewhat elusive and difficult and then one day it isn't. For now you'll do a little stumbling and grumbling — you'll do donuts, tangle the sheets and stop dead in the dead zone. But that's OK. Just don't go boom on the boom. That could ruin your whole day.

Ideally you want to work into an upwind course that goes from closehauled to a tack, closehauled to a tack, closehauled to a tack and so on — just like the zigzag diagrams. At first you may have a tendency to turn too far and tack into a reach. It'll take awhile to get your rhythm down, but with practice you'll be a Tackmeister Supreme.

Caught in irons

Let's say in your tack you become stuck in the dead zone. That is, the boat is pointed straight into the wind, the sails are luffing like crazy, and you're not moving anywhere. Using another (rather imaginative) phrase, you are *caught in irons*. This is a common enough occurrence and easy to remedy.

Just push the rudder all the way over and push out the boom so that the wind can hit the sail. The boat will back into a point of sail from which you can regain momentum and try the tack again.

Chapter 10:
Docking

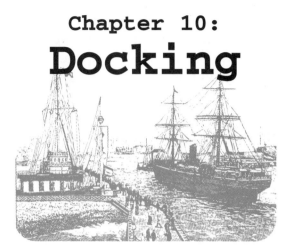

Well look at you! You can sail north and south, east and west, no matter which way the wind blows! So what if you're a little ragged. Where are the lanes out there, anyway? Where's the doggone road for that matter? Let's go back and do a little braggadocio!

Uh, oh. It's time to dock the boat!

This could be your worst moment. Prepare yourself. Nobody saw you sail so splendidly out there, but everybody's going to see you tear into the dock. Or miss it. Suffice it to say that docking your sailboat is one of those character building endeavors in life. Like the first time you tried to parallel park.

Docking is another timing thing. What you do is simple. Exactly when you do it is another matter. However, if you read the wind properly, chances are you'll do fine.

Figure out which way the wind is blowing to your dock. You want to end the glide into the dock going upwind. Barely moving. Never, ever try to land with the wind. You'll crash and burn for sure.

 Eyeball the place you want to be on the dock and **aim for a spot two boat lengths downwind**.

As you approach, **let the sails completely out.**

When you hit your spot, turn upwind and gently slide into the dock.

Obviously, it's better to have too little momentum than too much. Someone can always throw you a rope or you can try again if you fall short. But crashing is, well, crashing.

Before you set out, ask a local sailor the best way to deal with the dock. Each one has its own nuances.

My favorite docking story
Docking sailboats can be a hassle but as long as you avoid doing this one thing, chances are it won't be a catastrophe: **Do not attempt to dock under full sail.** It's like easing into a parking place at 40 miles an hour.

I had my first boat for about, oh, two weeks and had fallen in love with it and with sailing. Up to this point in time, I had never dealt with a dock, always having launched and landed from a beach. But on this day I was leaving from and returning to a dock. The leaving was a piece of cake. It was the arriving that became epic.

1 Docking — Sailing in slowly with sails out.

2 Turning upwind into the docking area.

3 Sheets are released.

4 Sliding gently next to the dock.

Not knowing that there might be a trick to this docking business, I was returning from a short jaunt in the bay on a reach with a moderate wind. I have no idea what I was thinking at the time. It didn't register that there might be a problem until I was practically on top of the dock.

Thoughts like *Gee, I'm going kinda fast. How am I going stop this thing?* flashed through my mind before it shut down entirely and I was forced to react to the impending danger with jungle reflexes alone.

With the dock looming in front of me, I cranked my craft alongside the dock at about 75 miles per hour, looped my feet under the hiking strap in the cockpit, lunged toward one of the pilings speeding by, and hugged it with all my might.

It was like Buster Keaton. Or more accurately, like some sort of cartoon because I'm sure I was stretching like Gumby.

I'm holding on to the piling with my arms and barely hanging on to this bucking boat with my toenails. I'm bridged over about five feet of water, losing my grip, and hoping nobody is witnessing all this — when the cavalry came.

It was Rich Gleason, owner of said dock, and sailing mentor-to-be. He grabbed the boat, uncleated the sail and reeled me in. Afterward, in that easy-going way of his, he explained that I *should* have approached the dock *into* the wind, or upwind, with sails loose. And quite a bit slower.

A good docking — This photo illustrates much about docking. As the boat approaches the dock the bow is pointed upwind and both sheets are released. The boat is moving just fast enough to park itself.

We both agreed that it was time for a little instruction.

This story illustrates the need to know something about the ways of the wind before you wing it. When thrashing about in the open water you can gain considerable wisdom through trial and error without serious consequence — in fact, that's a great way to learn 95% of this stuff. But when around other boats or the dock it's time for control. And in order to have control, a sailor needs to master basic skills.

Second, everyone makes mistakes! That's how you learn. Don't let embarrassments deter you from getting better and enjoying the experience.

Chapter 11:
Rules of the road

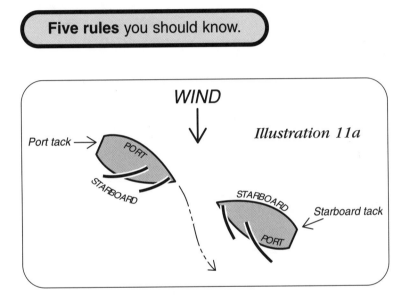

Illustration 11a

1. Starboard rule *(Illustration 11a)*
If two boats approach each other from opposite directions, the boat on a starboard tack has right of way over the boat on a port tack.

A starboard tack is when the wind blows into (over) your starboard (right) side. A port tack is when the wind blows into (over) your port (left) side. There is no particular reason for the starboard tack to supersede the port tack.

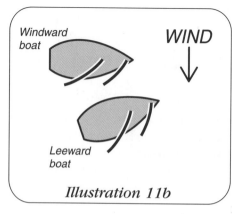

Windward boat

WIND

Leeward boat

Illustration 11b

2. Windward/ leeward rule

If two boats are traveling in the same direction, the leeward boat has right of way over the windward boat.

The windward boat is the boat the wind hits first. The leeward boat is the boat the wind hits after the windward boat.

There is a reason for this rule. The windward boat has more wind to work with than the leeward boat. Since the windward boat is receiving wind first it may be blocking the wind from the leeward boat. Thus, the windward boat has more control.

Windward, by the way, is pronounced like it looks. Leeward, however, is pronounced loo-erd. But the word "lee" by itself is pronounced lee, just like it looks.

This is yet another example of The Code. Why loo for lee with -erd, and lee for lee without? No reason. But watch the eyebrows pop if you say lee-ward instead of loo-erd.

3. Overtaking rule

If two boats are headed in the same direction, the slower boat has right of way. The overtaking boat gives way to the overtaken boat. The faster boat is assumed to have more control.

Outta the way!

4. Power boat rule

All power boats, 65 feet long or less, must give way to sailboats. Power boats have more control than a sailboat up to a point. When they get closer to aircraft carrier size, they do not. That means you get out of their way!

5. Courtesy rule

Even if you have right of way, you must avoid the other boat. In other words, don't run into anybody. Please remember this one. In fact, for now, just stay away from everybody and everything.

The bridge that wouldn't budge

Know the rules ... know the road!

A friend of mine was sailing an inland waterway in Florida for the first time when his fellow sailor pointed out a drawbridge ahead. The bridge seemed a little low for the mast and it was probable that the bridge would have to be drawn up in order for them to pass.

Ahead of them was a much larger vessel. It most certainly would need the bridge to lift. My friend and his mate watched to see how the first boat dealt with the situation.

As it closed in, they heard three sharp blasts from a horn and like *Open Sesame!* the bridge lifted and let the boat pass. In a minute or so the bridge came back down.

No problemo. Toot the horn thrice and the gates open. Got it.

In time their sailboat was upon the bridge. They tooted the horn and prepared to whisk on through.

The bridge didn't budge.

They blasted three more times. Not a crack.

Meanwhile, of course, their boat was getting mighty close to the bridge. And sure enough, the mast was a good five feet taller than the underpass. Now this sailboat was pretty big and pretty expensive. Masts on these puppies cost a mint. Breaking one tends to dampen the spirits of yachtsmen in no small way. And from the looks of things that's exactly what was in store unless some superior seamanship commenced pronto.

With his buddy blasting nonstop on the air horn, yelling and waving at the bridgemaster's hut, my pal cranked the boat around and desperately tried to high-tail it back before the mast hit. Needless to say, since sailboats can't respond to directional changes like a power boat, the situation was going to be tight.

With the mast inches from destruction and both sailors in a frenzied praying-cursing-accusing mode, the drawbridge decided to raise. Mast and boat glided through. Unscathed.

When there is no traffic you don't have to worry so much about rules. In the beginning it's best to look for clear and open water.

As they floated through to the other side, they noticed
a sign on the bridge:

DRAWBRIDGE OPENS AUTOMATICALLY EVERY 15
MINUTES. LISTEN FOR 3 HORN BLASTS.

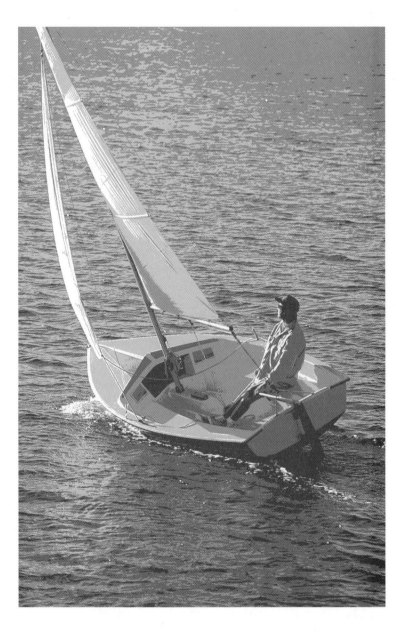

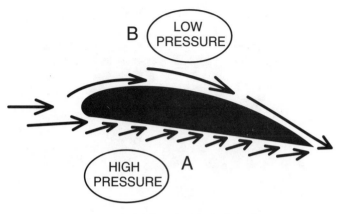

AIRPLANE WING

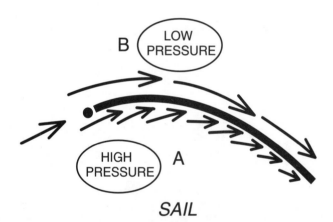

SAIL

Illustration 12a

Bernoulli Principle — Moving air splits itself above and below foil shapes. Air below the foils becomes condensed and creates high pressure systems that push into the low pressure areas above. This gives the wing its lift and your sail its shove.

Chapter 12:
Physics

What makes a sailboat go is a little more than wind pushing against the sails. It gets very technical with a multimillion dollar vessel, but for our purposes there are just a couple feats of physics we'll get into.

A sail is a foil *(Illustration 12a)*
The only time a sail acts as a wind catcher — when the wind is simply pushing sail and boat along — is when the boat is running with the wind. In any other direction (except the dead zone) a sail functions as a foil — pretty much like an airplane wing.

Pictured are a sail (from above), and an airplane wing (from the side). Around each is a flow of air particles. The flow around the sail is caused by the wind. The flow around the wing is caused by the movement of the airplane through the air. In both cases the air particles are split by either the leading edge of the sail (the mast), or the wing. As illustrated here, some of the particles go over the sail and wing (the B particles), and some go under (the A particles).

In both diagrams the B particles have a longer distance to travel than the A particles. This is due to the curving back of the foil shape around which they are traveling. These particles are less condensed than the A particles, which are getting jammed along the opposite side. All this jamming creates a higher pressure on this side than the other. It's this higher pressure on one side, in combination with the lower pressure on the other, that provides the push on the sail and the lift on a wing.

This is called the Bernoulli Principle — after Daniel Bernoulli, an eighteenth century Swiss physician, mathematician and physicist.

Sail angles

It follows that the angle of the sail can play an important role in all this particle pressure. As a sailor pulls in his sails on a reach, for example, he or she increases the pressure on the windward side of the sails and decreases the pressure on the leeward side. The result is increased boat speed and perhaps a pronounced tilt to lee.

Of course, there is a point where these physics are lost if the sailor pulls the sails in too much. There is an optimum setting for any point of sail.

Conversely, letting out the sails decreases the pressure on the windward side of the sails and results in a loss of speed.

Now all of this means nothing if you haven't got a daggerboard or centerboard.

Daggerboard or centerboard

The daggerboard or centerboard plays an integral role in moving your sailboat in all directions except downwind. Like I said, when the boat is moving downwind, the physics of motion is merely that of the wind pushing boat and sail. No foil. No split particles. No high or low pressures. You're just being shoved. That's why it's so slow.

The centerboard prevents the wind from pushing the boat leeward (with the wind) when the boat is pointed anywhere else. On a reach the wind hits the sail and boat broadside, but can't shove the boat that way because the centerboard pins the boat down. It makes the boat go in the direction the rudder tells it — the path of least resistance. Take the daggerboard out on a reach and the boat will blow with the wind. Without a daggerboard or centerboard a boat can only be sailed with the wind.

That's why you need some of this theory stuff.

Unless you design rockets for a living, it takes a wrenching of the brain muscle to plow through some of the finer points. I figured if I tried to explain the whys behind the hows all at once, folks would either doze off or start to weep uncontrollably. Especially when you're expecting light reading about fun boat rides.

Not to worry. Knowing theory won't sail your boat. Some is good to know, and it can be interesting in a left-side-of-the-brain kind of way. But it's better to get out there and plow around as soon as you can. It's the seeing and feeling and doing that'll pull you through. And those things won't happen sitting in a classroom.

Chapter 13:
Rigging
and knots

If you're renting your sailboat chances are you won't have to set it up or rig it. However, sooner or later you're going to have to learn. It's a step-by-step thing. Not very difficult at all.

At this point assume the boat is in the water, the mast is raised and secured by its wire shrouds.

1 Plug in the plug at the stern.

2 Slip in the centerboard next. It helps to stabilize the boat as you stumble on, off, and around it during the rigging ritual.

3 Attach the rudder to the pins on the outside of the stern. Make sure it passes underneath the ropes back there that attach to the boom (the traveler). Secure it with the rope or cord attachment.

4 Untie or unclasp the main halyard from the end of the boom. Unfurl the mainsail and attach the halyard to the tiptop of the mainsail. Use a bowline knot if there isn't a shackle.

5 Make sure the mainsheet is uncleated. Look up and check your main halyard for tangles or fouling. As you pull up the mainsail, feed the luff into the slot on the mast. Pull the sail all the way up and tie down your end of the halyard to the cleat at the base of the mast. Use a cleat knot. Coil the remaining rope and stuff it between the mast and halyard.

6 Look at your mainsail and check for sagging along the mast and boom. It should be pulled tight. If you need to adjust the tension along the boom, use the outhaul line located on the boom. If tension along the mast is lacking, use the downhaul line located at the base of the mast.

7 Unwrap the jib and attach the bottom to the hook on the bow. Starting at the bottom, fasten the little jib doohickies to the forestay.

8 Now take the jib sheets around the shrouds. One on each side of the boat, of course. Poke the ends of each through the cleats and tie them in figure-eight knots. Don't cleat them down.

9 Untie the jib halyard at the mast and attach the shackle to the tiptop of the jib sail. Pull the jib all the way up until the forestay is slightly slack. Cleat the jib halyard with a cleat knot on its cleat at the base of the mast. (Say THAT fast a few times.)

There you go! You should be ready to make sailing history. Make sure all your lines are coiled and stowed out of the way, that you have knots at the end of all your sheets, and that everything that you fiddled with is tied down tight. In other words, make sure you're ship-shape, mate.

Rigging makes sense
Your boat may very well be different than the one we rigged here. You might not have a jib. Or shrouds. Some stuff isn't going to attach or tie down or look exactly like it's shown and described here.

But a lot of it should be similar. Or similar enough for you to piece together a small monohull of most any type without too much fret and sweat. Obviously, advice and real-live instruction is always a good idea if it continues to be a jumble.

And do remember this. Everything about rigging makes perfect sense. Always. No matter what boat. It's one of the beauties of sailing. Perhaps the jargon is somewhat confusing and convoluted, but the way your little boat is meant to be put together is precise. And once understood, simple.

Rigging — Plug the plug   Slide in the daggerboard.

Attach rudder.   Unclasp the main halyard (rope that pulls up the main sail) from the boom.

5

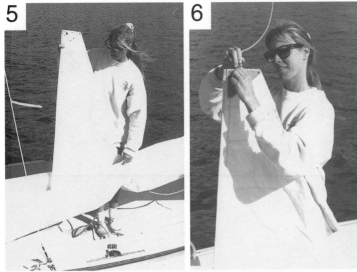

Unfurl mainsail.

6

Attach main halyard to top of mast.

7

Check for tangles.

8

Slide mainsail into the slot on the mast.

Haul up the mainsail, making sure the mainsheet is uncleated.

Cleat the main halyard. See page 90 for knot.

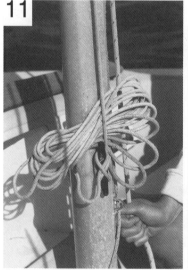

Neatly coiled and stowed.

Check for sagging along boom and mast.

13

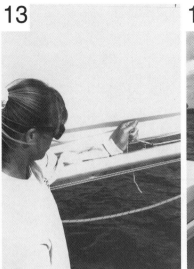

Adjust outhaul for sagging along the boom.

14

Adjust downhaul for sagging along the mast.

15

Hook bottom of jib to bow.

16

Fasten jib to forestay (the wire stretching from bow to top of mast.

17

Jib sheets go around the shrouds (wires holding up mast) ...

18

... and through their respective cleats. Tie ends in figure-eight knots. See page 91 for knot. Do not cleat.

19

Attach jib halyard to top of jib.

20

Haul up the jib.

Check it out — Step back and take a look. Sails should be pulled all the way up and out. No sagging.

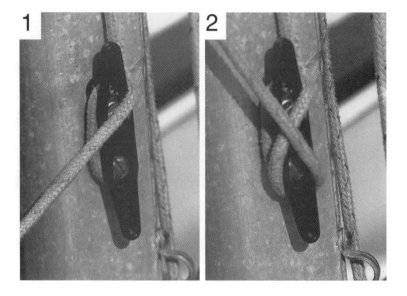

Cleat knot — For cleating the halyard.

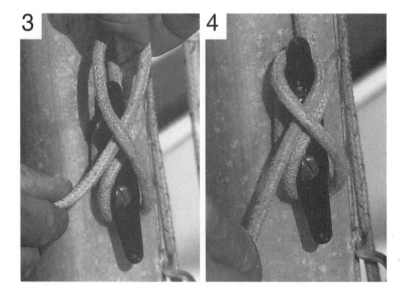

Figure-eight knot — For tying off the jib sheets.

Bowline — For attaching a line to anything. It does not slip.

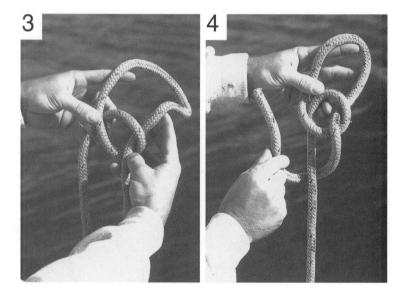

Chapter 14:
Safety

Be aware, be prepared and use common sense.
Respect the elements and sail within your skill level.

1. Let someone know when you are leaving and when you are returning.

2. Know how to swim.

3. Make sure vessel and gear are sound.

4. Know the waters.
- Look at a chart of the area before setting out.
- Be aware of your draft (how deep your boat is) and the depth of the water.
- Avoid rocks, shallow water, strong currents or a lee shore (shore that the wind is blowing into).

5. Know the rules of the road *(Chapter 11)* and the boating laws in your area.

6. Know your limitations: Don't sail boats or in weather that you cannot handle.

7. Check the local marine weather forecast.

8. Stay with a capsized boat.

9. Use navigation lights if you sail at night.

10. Watch out for the boom.

11. Watch where you are going.

Safety gear checklist
- [ ] Life jacket for each person on board
- [ ] Sunglasses
- [ ] Sunscreen
- [ ] Whistle or horn
- [ ] Bailer (something to scoop out water)
- [ ] Paddle
- [ ] Floatable cushion or ring with line
- [ ] Wristwatch

For longer trips
- [ ] Plenty of drinking water
- [ ] Two extra lengths of line — one short and one long (15 to 20 feet)
- [ ] Tool bag with screwdriver, pliers, extra tack pin and shackle, rigging knife (loosens knots and shackles), marline (tarred twine) and duct tape
- [ ] First-aid kit
- [ ] Anchor
- [ ] Compass

Chapter 15:
Bligh
syndrome

Captain Bligh — The Cap'n who gave Clark Gable, Marlon Brando, and later Mel Gibson such a rough time on the HMS Bounty.)

In the movie *Overboard* starring Goldie Hawn there is a scene that illustrates a certain behavioral problem associated with seamanship. The film is a comedy and among other things touches upon the relationship between a rich yachtsman (Edward Herrmann) and his wife (Goldie) who are embarking on a world cruise.

In this scene he is at the helm of his boat and having a fierce argument with Goldie. The fight escalates to a point where he threatens to toss her overboard. She laughs and says *You wouldn't dare!* His response is classic Bligh:

I'll do whatever I want — at sea a Captain is GOD!

It was meant to be funny, of course, but like a lot humor it touches close to something that isn't very funny at all when one is on the receiving end.

Anyone who has ever sailed knows exactly what I'm talking about. It has something to do with the tiller. Whomever touches it becomes *Captain*. If he (or she) is allowed to keep it for any length of time, a personality change ensues that in stages becomes blunt, gruff, and finally mad dog. In no time at all an otherwise docile human being will become an Ahab. An Admiral Nelson. A Captain Blood. And woe to the hapless crew!

It reminds me of that old Goofy cartoon. The one in which he's a mild-mannered family man until he gets behind the wheel of his car. There he turns into this raving lunatic — screeching and speeding his auto out of the neighborhood, blowing other cars off the road, screaming and shaking his fist until he pulls into his parking place at the office. He then retransforms himself into the gentle soul he normally is.

What is it about boats and madcaps, anyway? Why do everyday nice people turn into such fanatics on the high seas? Maybe it's the confined space. Maybe it's too many Errol Flynn movies. Maybe they just think they can get away with it — as if the open waters are some kind of frontier where civilized behavior is optional. Whatever the reason, many a sailing sortie has turned ugly because the captain got fat in the head.

Like the Code and barnacles, Bligh syndrome isn't going away soon. Try to avoid:

1. Anyone dressed in a blue blazer, matching white turtleneck and trousers, and yachting cap. This indicates a troubled mind, but if his boat is only 14-feet long, you know you're dealing with chronic Bligh.

2. Anyone drinking gin out of the bottle before 10 a.m.

3. Anyone rattling ball bearings.

4. Anyone wearing a saber and a Napoleon bonnet.

The list goes on, yet it's the normal-looking ones, the people you know and trust, who'll get you every time. And here's the grabber — *there is nothing you can do about it!*

As long as you accept boat rides on other people's boats, you are at risk. As long as you remain a novice to the sailing game, you will be at the mercy of those demented individuals who grow horns at the tiller.

You must take this sailing business to heart and learn how to skipper your own boat. Then *you* can set the rules. Then you can be the sensitive, caring, patient captain that everyone will admire and point to and say *There's the skipper who isn't a jerk!*

Or you can be your own Bligh — and seek vengeance like the rest of us.

Big sails plus light hulls equal speed!

Chapter 16:
Catamarans

Maybe you are getting itchy.

You've seen the ads with the guy hanging w-a-a-a-y out over the water sailing a boat that looks a lot different than your sloop. The boat is nearly upended and it's tracking at warp speed. You want to try one of those.

Catamarans or cats are probably what you have in mind. As previously mentioned, catamarans have two hulls (usually). On any given day, they're the fastest sailboats in the water. As a matter of fact, cats can speed up to 25 knots. That's twice as fast as the sleekest monohull. The little boat you learned in can only go three knots.

The physics behind all this mostly involves sail area and boat weight. Cats are relatively light and have huge sails. Monohulls are heavier. Cats get moving so fast that they create their own wind.

Go ahead and try one out — right after you read ...

Catamaran qualifier for beginners
You have enough knowledge and skill at this point to
manage or begin to learn to manage a catamaran in
light to moderate wind. That's about eight knots or less.
You should be able to take off, come back in, locate
and negotiate the points of sail including tacking (the
wind circle applies just the same) — even fly a hull,
without much problem.

But stay away from heavier winds. Cats really tear in
and out of the water. They are built to charge. It takes a
little more know-how than you have at this time to
safely address anything more than a stiff breeze.

What's different about cats?
Your initial cat rides will probably be on a 16- or
18-foot boat. These are the most common sizes.

Besides the two skinny hulls (that you'll want to call
pontoons — but don't) other differences include:

1. Getting wet
Prepare for a dousing spray and butt soaks.

2. Awright! No docks!
Taking off from and landing on the beach. They're
made to do just that. Usually that's how you'll find
them at sailing areas.

3. What! No seats?
No seats or sides. Cats have a trampoline-like platform
(called a trampoline) made of stretched canvas upon
which you'll scramble and sit. There are straps to scoot
feet under and not much of anything else.

Catamarans are made to park on the beach.

Catamarans have long tillers to reach hiking, scrambling sailors ...

4. No centerboard
The function of a centerboard is incorporated into the hull design of a cat.

5. Two rudders
One behind each hull. There's a bar contraption or rope dealies that pop them up and down. When you smash into the beach they'll pop up without damage.

6. A long, cumbersome pole
The tiller is a long pole. You fit it under your armpit. It can be awkward during a tack because of the length. You have to swing it out and around each time you change sides. It's long so you can always have a hold of it as you move around.

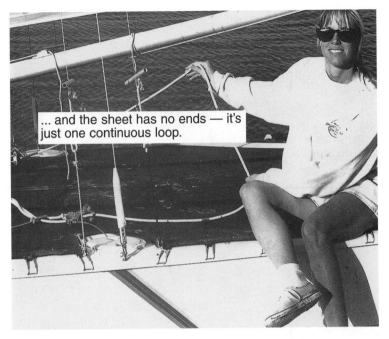

... and the sheet has no ends — it's just one continuous loop.

7. Endless sheets

The sails are managed the same as your monohull's. It's just that the sheet has no ends. It's one big loop of rope that run through the cleats. No loose ends.

8. Trimming

It's pretty much the same as before. Pull 'em in and let 'em out. You'll find that in a cat the sails will want to be pulled in closer when you're closehauled and on broad reaches than in a monohull.

9. It's so <u>fast!</u>

Once you've pushed off, set the sails and caught a little wind, you'll notice the *difference* right away. Make no mistake about it — cats are built for speed.

10. Yeah! It's **really** fun!

You're so close to the water — you can see it rushing beneath you through the webbing of the trampoline. And since there aren't any sides, it's like your on this speeding carpet ride. Without a doubt, cats are the sexy, sizzling, hotdogging side of small boat sailing.

11. Flying a hull

Get set in a reach. If there's enough wind, your windward hull (the one you're sitting over) will want to rise out of the water. And up you'll go! Tearing along on one hull, balancing just so that you maintain maximum trim and thrust (hull is 3 to 6 inches out of the water) is one of the major thrills in cat sailing.

It's also a workout. The mainsail is big, catches a lot of wind and is tough to sheet in. The boat is going so fast that maintaining a bearing on a maxed-out reach is like wrestling a baby rhino. And you thought sailing was a finesse sport!

Remember, *when in doubt, let 'em out!* If it feels like you're going to be catapulted, just let out the mainsail like you did in the monohull.

12. Downwind sailing
Running directly with the wind in a cat is slow. You do it just like you did in the monohull.

It's faster to sail toward your bearing in a series of broad reaches, again, like you did in the sloop. Even though your zigzag course is much longer than a straight run, your cat will cover the distance in much shorter time.

13. Capsizing
This is a major hassle. You can't right the boat by yourself. It takes 325 pounds and a tussle to get a cat back upright. If you stay out of strong winds and monitor your mainsail properly you should be fine. But here's what you do if you end-o (illustrated next two pages):

a. Uncleat the sheets.

b. Locate the righting rope underneath the trampoline.

c. Toss the rope over the upended hull.

d. Both sailors grab hold, stand on the bottom hull and pull! The cat will plop over and settle over your heads.

14. Tacking
This one deserves its own chapter ...

Capsize recovery — After releasing the sheets, Cliff tosses the righting rope over the upended hull ...

... and catches it on the other side.

Cliff and Tom start pulling.

Keep pulling ...

... and pulling ...

... until the sails burst free of the water.

The cat rights itself and plops safely over their heads.

Chapter 17:
Tacking in a cat

This you will have to relearn. Tacking is slow going in a cat. They're not built to come about quickly or efficiently. In fact, the hassle in coming about in a cat is not coming about at all, or getting stuck in the dead zone (caught in irons).

Cat tacking step by step:

1 **Achieve a closehauled course.** You want the cat to have as little distance to swing around as possible. When a cat isn't going in a straight line it just wants to squat and die.

2 **Push the tiller away slowly** and don't let go. Cats do not respond well to abrupt directional change. It'll stop. Of course, if the tiller isn't held to a steady course the boat will cease its pivot.

Do not release the sheets, yet.

3 As the boat swings around **the jib will begin to pick up the wind** from the other side and help push you all the way around. This is called backwinding. It's more or less the jib that does the work in a cat tack.

4 **Release the mainsheet and switch sides.**
Remember to hold on to the tiller and to keep it
turned the way you want to go. It's easy to lose control
because of the long-poled tiller — it has to swing out,
around and underneath the boom. It's awkward, but
since the tack is so slow you should have plenty of
fumbling time.

5 **The mainsail will pop!** as it fills with wind.
Grab hold of the mainsheet.

6 **Release the jib** (at last) and **set it on the other
side** of the boat.

And away you'll go. Or perhaps I should say *zoom!* Cats
are definitely off-track on a tack, but point them in the
right direction and you're flying in no time.

Take note that the mainsail is dormant throughout the
tack. If it becomes involved too soon it'll counteract
the push upon the jib and spin you back.

You will get stuck in the dead zone more frequently in
a cat than in a monohull. If you get caught in irons,
push the rudder over and push the boom out as you
did in the sloop. You'll back out of the stall into a point
of sail from which you can try another tack.

It's this tacking business that requires the most
schooling when you graduate from monohull to catamaran (up to this point, anyway.) As you progress and
deal with greater wind there will be much more to
absorb.

Critical moment during a tack — moving past the dead zone waiting for the jib to pick up the wind and finish the turn.

Tacking in a cat

Cat tack — Cliff and Connie prepare to tack after a close-hauled course.

Cliff slowly pushes the tiller away.

Slowly the boat comes around.

The cat is pointed directly into the dead zone. The jib picks up the wind.

5

It's the jib that helps complete the tack at this point. The mainsheet is released and sailors switch sides.

6

Mr. Jib still works away while the mainsail remains dormant. Cliff cranks the tiller out and around maintaining the turn.

7

Cliff and Connie settle in and wait for the mainsail to catch wind.

8

With a POP! it finally does. Connie releases the jib sheet and sets it on the other side. Cliff has hold of the mainsheet and prepares to take off.

Chapter 18:
How cats go

Big sails on a **light hull** equals **speed.**

And all this speed makes for what is called created wind — like the wind your car makes when it speeds forward. Stick your hand out and you feel created wind. Your monohull's forward progress wasn't great enough to produce much.

Here comes the theory part *(Illustration 18a, next page)*. The mean between the real wind (as in where the natural wind is blowing from), and the created wind (the wind blowing over the bow as you move), is called apparent wind. Apparent wind is the distillation of real and created wind that actually reacts with your cat's sails and makes you move.

See the angle of the apparent wind as it hits your cat?
It's much sharper than the angle the real wind made
against your monohull sail. Apparent wind is more
straight on.

In order for a sail to work in apparent wind, it must be
less foiled, or flatter than a monohull's sail *(Illustration
18b, next page)*. The straight-on nature of apparent
wind will buckle the foil of a bulging monohull sail and
render it a flapping, useless mess. In order to flatten cat
sails, battens are strung all the way through the width
of the sail. This makes them stiff enough to hold their
flat shape as well. It's this stiffness that makes a cat's
sail Pop! when you tack.

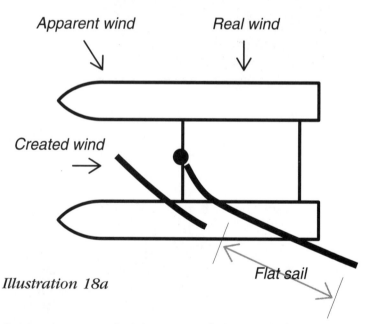

Illustration 18a

Catamarans are so fast they create their own wind — apparent
wind. Cat sails are flatter and less foiled than monohull sails in
order to deal with the angle of apparent wind.

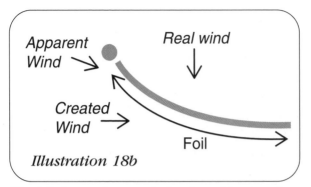

Apparent Wind

Real wind

Created Wind

Foil

Illustration 18b

The foil shape of a monohull sail would not work on a cat. Apparent wind would buckle the foil and render it useless.

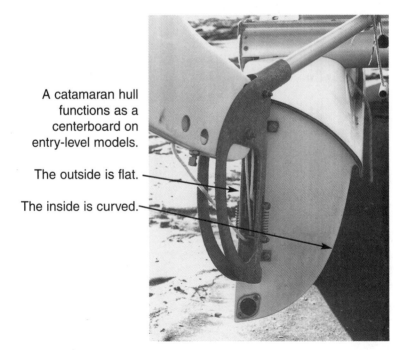

A catamaran hull functions as a centerboard on entry-level models.

The outside is flat.

The inside is curved.

No centerboard
The outside of each hull is flat. The design functions like the centerboard in a monohull.

Maximum trim
... is achieved when one hull is in the water and the other is 3 to 6 inches out. One hull in the water is less resistant than two. But going too high prevents the wind from reacting with the sail at an optimum angle.

Maximum trim also requires that the waterline around your hull(s) is even. Avoid having your hull(s) dip down (pitch-pulling) or ride up. You balance things by placing your weight properly and monitoring the main-sail.

Tacking
Tacking is slow going because one of the hulls is resisting the movement. Instead of one hull pivoting and turning, a cat has one hull pivoting and the other trying to pivot around it.

Easy does it!
Cat sailing isn't easy. Or it's easy until it isn't and then all hell breaks loose. This chapter is meant to whet your appetite. That's all. Take lessons and learn from a pro. Yeah, you can give it a go in light winds, but catamarans can get really spooky and scary when it starts to blow. Know your limitations!

Zoned

I'll never forget the first time I took a catamaran out in the ocean. The wind was light on the bay as we sailed toward the inlet. So light we barely made it to sea.

Once in the inlet, the swells marched underneath us like a bunch of rolling hills. Gently bucking us up and down. Then way up and way down. The open ocean was starting to look and feel real BIG.

Then the wind hit. Outside the protected bay the prevailing wind had nothing to slow it down. Away we went! — like zero to sixty in five seconds. The sails popped and the boat actually started to hum. The hull we were sitting over lifted and we assumed that hanging-over-the-side position you see in all the magazines — without even thinking about it.

I was mesmerized by the power. The hulls cut through the chop like a speedboat. Looking back, each rudder was spewing a rooster tail. Holding on to sheet and tiller was a job for Atlas.

We got going so fast that the boat bolted practically upright. I slid down the trampoline, underneath the hiking strap, up to my armpits. For a second or two we were sailing on end with me in this semi-crucifix position and my buddy sitting *on the side* of the uplifted hull. It certainly felt like curtains. In the nick of time I managed to let out the main and we plopped back down.

What a ride! After a while I got a feel for the lift of the hull together with the proper sail tension — balancing just so in order to maintain this hair-raising thrust through the water. Man, I was in the zone! I never dreamed that sailing could be such a rip-roaring, limb-wrenching, roller-coaster ride!

Different strokes

Now obviously catamaran sailing isn't for everybody. And I'm sure that after reading the previous ditty many of you will begin to ascertain your own feelings about high performance sailing. Some of you are going to water at the mouth and give it a try. But many of you will want to pass. And that's OK.

Because this is a fact: If there's a sport with variety, it's sailing. It can be fast or slow, thrilling or laid-back, wet or dry or anything you want it to be. And somewhere there's a boat just for you to do those very things. Guaranteed.

One more thing about sailing — there's always something else to learn. All this is just scratching the surface. There's a zillion different boats and a zillion different ways to sail them. Every time you go out there's a different set of conditions to challenge you. So keep at it and have some fun out there. After all, that's what sailing is all about!

Glossary

A sailing glossary could easily fill a book. What you have here is pretty much what you should know.

Aft — A part of the boat at or near the stern.
Apparent wind — Associated with catamaran sailing. The mean between real and created wind.

Backwinding — When caught in irons, pushing boom and mainsail out in order to catch wind and move back into a point of sail.
Battens — The thin strips of wood or fiberglas that fit into and stiffen sails.
Bearing — The point a sailor chooses to sail toward.
Bernoulli principle — A major part of sailing theory and physics. Explains how a sail works. Daniel Bernoulli (1700-1782) was a Swiss physician, mathematician and physicist.
Boom — The wood or metal beam attached to the mast and mainsail.
Bow — The front of the boat.
Bowline — A common knot in sailing. Noteworthy in that it never slips.
Broad reach — A direction or point of sail 135 degrees from the wind source.

Catamaran — A boat with two or more hulls.
Cat — Catamaran.
Capsize — To overturn a boat.
Caught in irons — When the bow is pointed upwind and the boat cannot move forward or turn.

Centerboard — A hinged stabilizing member located underneath the hull.

Cleat — A fitting used to secure lines.

Cleat knot — The knot used to tie lines to cleats.

Closehauled — Describes the direction or point of sail 45 degrees from the wind source.

Created wind — The wind created from forward movement associated with catamaran sailing.

Daggerboard — A stabilizing member located underneath the hull that slides in and out.

Dead zone — That direction 45 degrees to either side of the wind source in which sailing is impossible. Also luffing zone or no sail zone.

Downhaul — The line that adjusts vertical tension in the mainsail.

Downwind — A direction with the wind, away from the wind source.

Flying a hull — When one hull of a catamaran lifts up and out of the water, usually on a reach.

Fore — A part of a boat at or near the bow.

Forestay — The wire mast support attached to the bow.

Halyard — The line that hauls up the sail.

Hull — The body of the boat.

Jib sail — The smaller sail attached to the bow.

Jibing — Turning with the wind on a downwind course by pulling the tiller in or away from the sail(s).

Knot — A nautical unit of speed equaling 1.15 mph.

Laser — Make of a small, single-sail boat known for its maneuverability.

Leeward — Pronounced loo-erd. Situated or moving away from the wind source.

Luff — Leading edge of a sail. Also a verb — the flapping of untrimmed sails.

Mainsail — The bigger sail attached to the boom.

Mast — The big pole holding up the sails.

Monohull — A boat with a single hull.

Outhaul — The line that adjusts the horizontal tension on the mainsail.

Pitch-pulling — When the bow of a catamaran dips below the surface.

Point of sail — A sailing direction with specific trimming requirements.

Port tack — When the wind blows over the port (left) side of the boat.

Port — Left as a sailor faces forward toward the bow.

Reach — The direction or point of sail 90 degrees from the wind source.

Real wind — The true, natural wind as opposed to created or apparent wind.

Rigging — Setting up a boat, making ready for sail.

Rudder — The turning blade in the water, at the stern, attached to the tiller.

Run — The direction or point of sail 180 degrees from the wind source.

Sheet — The line used to control the sail.

Shrouds — The wire mast supports attached to the sides of the boat.

Sloop — A sailboat with a jib and mainsail.

Starboard — Right as a sailor faces forward toward the bow.

Starboard tack — When the wind blows over the starboard (right) side.

Stern — The back of the boat.

Tacking — Turning into the wind on an upwind course by pushing the tiller away or toward the sail(s).

Telltails — The strips of fabric attached to sails or shrouds indicating wind direction.

Tiller — The steering handle attached to the rudder.

Trampoline — The stretched canvas platform upon which sailors sit on catamarans.

Trimming — Adjusting sail tension by pulling in or letting out the sheets.

Upwind — A direction against the wind, toward the wind source.

Wind circle — The circular diagram universally used to explain the points of sail.

Windward — Situated or moving toward the wind source.

Resources

Sailing centers, dealers, rental outlets, schools and stores are places to meet people who know about sailing. Look in the yellow pages under "Boats" or "Boating" ("Sailing" may not work — it doesn't in San Diego, of all places).

Since first you'll want to get instruction and rent, your best bet is probably a rental outlet that provides lessons. Folks at these places are also used to dealing with neophytes and answering questions is just part of the job. There you should be able to accumulate local information about:

Sailing areas
Sailing museums
Sailing instruction
Sailing organizations
Sailing conditions

Of course, these dockside operations will also provide:

Sailboats
Sailing literature
Sailing gear
Sailors to talk to

BOOKS

Chances are your local library will have plenty of books about sailing. After all, it is an ancient activity.

Many sailing stores, outlets and centers will have a book section. Some are absolutely overwhelming. There are thousands of books about every aspect of sailing including boats, technique, navigation, safety, gear, weather, places to sail, rules, cooking, construction, knots, history — you name it. Sailing is one of those romantic lifestyle pursuits that people like to read and write about a great deal.

Here are three bibles of sailing. Each is a mother load of information:

The Annapolis Book of Seamanship; John Rousmaniere; Simon and Schuster, New York, New York, 1997; 402 pages, heavily illustrated. $29.95

Chapman Piloting, Seamanship and Small Boat Handling; Elbert S. Maloney; Hearst Marine Books, 1999; 656 pages, heavily illustrated. $45.00

Royce's Sailing Illustrated; Patrick M. Royce; Royce Publications, Newport Beach, California, 1997; 160 pages, heavily illustrated. $19.95

BASIC INSTRUCTIONAL BOOKS

The Complete Sailor; David Seidman; International Marine, Camden, Maine, 1995; 208 pages, heavily illustrated. $15.95
"An encyclopedic guide" for the advanced sailor.

Learning to Sail; Di Goodman; International Marine, Camden, Maine, 1994; 104 pages, simple line drawings, some photos. $12.95
Primer for Annapolis Sailing School.

Sailing for Dummies; Peter Isler; IDG Books, Foster City, California, 1997; 404 pages, line drawings and photos. $19.95
Large, comprehensive guide. Textbook style the "dummy way" with bulleted highlights.

Sailing Fundamentals; Gary Jobson and American Sailing Association; Simon & Schuster, New York, New York, 1998; 224 pages, line drawings and photos. $17.00
Textbook by and for American Sailing Association.

Start Sailing Right!; United States Sailing Association; Portsmouth, Rhode Island, 1997; 110 pages, simple line drawings. $14.95
Textbook style with summaries, review sections.
Textbook by and for United States Sailing Association.

MAGAZINES

Sail Magazine
84 State Street
Boston, MA 02109-2202
671-720-8606
Fax 617-723-0912
www.sailmag.com

Sailing Magazine
PO Box 249
Port Washington, WI 53074
262-284-3494
Fax 262-284-7764
sailing@execpc.com, www.sailnet/sailing

Sailing World
Cruising World
5 John Clarke Road
PO Box 3400
Newport, RI 02840-0992
401-845-5100
Fax 401-845-5180
www.sailingworld.com

ORGANIZATIONS

American Sailing Association
America's sail education authority
13922 Marquesas Way
Marina Del Ray, CA 90292
310-822-7171
www.asa.com

United States Sailing Association
National governing body of the sport of sailing
PO Box 1260
15 Maritime Drive
Portsmouth, RI 02871-0907
800-ussail1
401-683-0800 Fax 401-683-0840
www.ussailing.com

United States Coast Guard
Information on the Coast Guard Recreational Boating
Safety Program.
Dedicated to improving the knowledge, skills and abilities of recreational boaters with the ultimate goal of reducing the loss of life, injuries and property damage that occur on U.S. waterways.

www.uscgboating.org
800-368-5647 8 a.m. to 4 p.m. EST

United States Coast Guard Auxiliary
The civilian volunteer arm of the United States Coast
Guard. Information about boating safety classes, courtesy boat examinations and boating safety.
www.cgaux.org

United States Power Squadrons
*USPS is a nonprofit, educational organization dedi-
cated to making boating safer and more enjoyable
by teaching classes in seamanship, navigation and
related subjects.*

PO Box 30423
Raleigh, NC 27622
1-888-for-usps
www.usps.org

TELEVISION
When ESPN covered the America's Cup off Freemantle,
Australia in 1987, sailing came into the living rooms of
millions of viewers worldwide. In America the races
became an especially important issue because our team
had lost for the first time ever in 1983. The competition
became something of a crusade. When Dennis Conners
finally won the Cup, it was like V-J Day. The fact that it
was Conners who had lost in 1983 made the story
even more epic.

Outside of the scintillating plot, ESPN's brilliant camera
work brought the viewers into the boats and the races
themselves. It was probably one of the greatest promo-

tions for sailing in history.

The Cup only happens once every few years, but thanks to the wonderful world of cable, other sailing events are periodically aired. Check your listings.

ESPN sailing coverage
http://jobson.softstone.net/tvsched.html

VIDEOS
There are several videos to choose from. A couple of good ones for beginners are:

Learn to Sail
Steve Colgate (Bennet Marine Video).

The United States Power Squadron's Boating Course for Power and Sail
with the United States Coast Guard
(Hearst Marine Books). This one comes with a book.

John Rousmaniere has an advanced series of videos titled **The Annapolis Book of Seamanship Video Series** (Creative Programming, Inc.). They include:

Volume 1: Cruising Under Sail
Volume 2: Heavy Weather Sailing
Volume 3: Safety at Sea
Volume 4: Sailboat Navigation
Volume 5: Daysailers, Sailing and Racing

WEB SITES

Information and links
www-personal.umich.edu/~tmorris/boatsail.htm
Best sailing pages on the web
A major portal to all things sailing

These sites also offer links and information:
www.asa.com
American Sailing Association

www.cgaux.org
Coast Guard Auxiliary

www.sailingworld.com
Sailing World Magazine

www.sailmag.com
Sail Magazine

www.sailnet.com
Sailing resource

www.uscgboating.org
United States Coast Guard Boating Safety

www.ussailing.com
United States Sailing Association

Bibliography

Alexander, Stuart. Sail of the Century. Dobbs Ferry, New York, New York: Sheridan House, 1987.

Johnson, Peter. The Guinness Guide to Sailing. Middlesex, England: Guinness Superlatives Ltd., 1981.

Laing, Alexander. Seafaring America. New York, New York: American Heritage Publishing Co., Inc., 1974.

Morton, A. Harry. The Wind Commands. Middletown, Connecticut: Wesleyan University Press, 1975.

Index

Apparent wind 117-119

Backwinding
      Catamaran 111, 112
      Monohull 61, 62
Bernoulis principle 76-78
Bligh Syndrome 97-99
Boom 20, 21
Bow 20, 25
Broad reach 34, 36, 52, 53, 54, 105, 107

Capsizing
      Catamaran 107, 108-109
      Monohull 44-45, 46-47
Catamaran 17, 19, 101-109, 111-115, 117-122
Caught in irons 61, 62, 112
Centerboard 22, 79
Cleats 22
Closehauled 34, 35, 36, 56, 57, 58, 59, 60, 62, 105, 111, 114
Clothing 15
Conditions 29-31
Courtesy rule 71
Created wind 117, 118, 119

Daggerboard 22-23, 79
Dead zone 33, 34, 35, 53, 58, 59, 61
Docking 63-68
Downwind sailing 51-55, 107

Flying a hull 30, 106-107, 121

Hull
      Catamaran 119-120
      Monohull 20, 23

Jib 20, 21

Knots
      Cleat 90
      Figure-eight 91
      Bowline 92-93

Dock, leaving the 37-40
Leeward boat 70
Luff 20, 23, 40, 41

Mainsail 20, 21
Mast 20, 21
Monohull 17-19
      Parts of 21-27

Overtaking rule 70

Parts of boat
      Catamaran 102, 104-105, 119, 120
      Monohull 21-27
Physics
      Catamaran 117-120
      Monohull 77-80
Pitch pulling 120
Points of sail 34, 35, 36
Port 24, 25
Port tack 69
Power boat rule 71

Reach 34, 35, 36, 43-44
Real wind 117, 118, 119
Rigging 81-89
Rudder
    Catamaran 104
    Monohull 20, 23
Rules 69-71
Running 34, 36, 51, 52

Safety 95-96
Sails
    Catamaran 118
    Monohull 20, 21
Sail angles 78
Sheets
    Catamaran 105
    Monohull 20, 22, 23
Starboard 24, 25
Starboard rule 69
Starboard tack 70
Stern 20, 25

Tacking
    Catamaran 111-115, 120
    Monohull 35, 36, 57-62
Telltails 25
Tiller
    Catamaran 104
    Monohull 20, 23
Trampoline 102
Trimming
    Catamaran 105, 120
    Monohull 41-42

Upwind sailing 57-62

Whitecaps 30
Wind 30
Wind circle 34, 35, 36, 53
Windward boat 70
Windward/ leeward rule 70

Munns

About the author

Doug Werner is the author of the internationally acclaimed Start-Up Sports series. In previous lifetimes he graduated with a fine arts degree from Cal State Long Beach, built an ad agency and founded a graphics firm. In 1994 he established Tracks Publishing.

Werner lives with his wife Kathleen and daughter Joy in San Diego, California — one of the major sport fun-zones on the planet.

Ordering More
Start-Up Sports®
Books

The Start-Up Sports series includes guides on
surfing, snowboarding, sailing, in-line skating, roller
hockey, bowling, longboard surfing, golfing, fencing,
boxing and skateboarding.

Order by mail, phone or online.

Tracks Publishing
140 Brightwood Ave. Chula Vista, CA 91910
1-800-443-3570
www.startupsports.com